HOW TO START A BUSINESS:

GUIDE TO SUCCESS

© **Pd John**

Copyright

All rights reserved, it is not permitted to copy, reprint or duplicate this book without the permission of the author.

Major Prophet PD John
P.O. BOX 4016
Mwanza - Tanzania
Phone number:
+255 762 415 790/ +255 759 204 744
Yohanayona3@gmail.com
www.hl centre.info

ISBN : 9798328918312
First edition ©2024.
Imprint: Independently published

Chief Editor:
Josia pd John
josiajohn735@gmail.com
Dar es salaam - Tanzania
Tel: +255 758588127/ +255 693522834

Dedication:

To all the aspiring entrepreneurs who dare to dream, who have the courage to take risks, and who are committed to turning their visions into reality. May this guide serve as your compass, guiding you through the uncharted waters of entrepreneurship. Your determination, creativity, and perseverance are the driving forces behind every innovation, every success, and every positive change in the world. May your journey be filled with growth, learning, and triumphs. Here's to your unwavering pursuit of success and your impact on shaping the future. This book is dedicated to you."

Preface:

Embarking on the journey of entrepreneurship is an exhilarating endeavor. It's a path that demands innovation, determination, and the willingness to challenge the status quo. This guide, 'How to Start a Business: Guide to Success,' is born out of the recognition that starting and growing a business is a complex and multifaceted journey, one that requires a blend of strategic thinking, practical insights, and an unyielding spirit.

The purpose of this book is to provide you, the aspiring entrepreneur, with a comprehensive roadmap that navigates the exciting and often unpredictable terrain of business creation. Whether you're at the inception of a groundbreaking idea, on the cusp of launching your venture, or navigating the complexities of scaling, this guide is designed to accompany you at every stage of your journey.

Through the following chapters, we'll explore the essentials of entrepreneurship, from cultivating the right mindset to crafting a solid business plan, from understanding legal and financial intricacies to launching and scaling your business successfully. We'll delve into real-world case studies, proven strategies, and expert advice to equip you with the knowledge and tools necessary to overcome challenges, seize opportunities, and achieve lasting success.

But remember, entrepreneurship is not just about profit; it's about impact. It's about solving problems, creating value, and leaving a positive mark on the world. As you navigate the pages of this guide, keep in mind that your journey is unique. Your business will be a reflection of your passion, your insights, and your determination.

Whether you're starting a small local venture or dreaming of disrupting industries on a global scale, your journey starts here. The path ahead may be challenging, but it's also incredibly rewarding. As you turn these pages and embark on your entrepreneurial odyssey, embrace the uncertainty, celebrate the victories, and never lose sight of the impact you can make.

With an open mind and an entrepreneurial spirit, let us embark on this journey together. Here's to your success, your growth, and your boundless potential."

[Prophet PD John]

Table of Contents

Copyright i

Dedication: ii

Preface: iii

Table of Contents vi

Part 1: The Entrepreneurial Mindset xiii

Chapter 1: Introduction to Entrepreneurship 1

    Entrepreneurship: A Journey of Creation and Innovation 1

    Overcoming Myths and Misconceptions 2

    Conclusion 4

Chapter 2: Cultivating the Entrepreneurial Mindset 5

    Developing an Entrepreneurial Mindset: Seeds of Success 5

    Navigating Risk and Uncertainty with Faith 7

Personal Testimony: Navigating Stormy Seas ..8

In Conclusion 8

Part 2: Ideation and Validation 10

Chapter 3: Generating Business Ideas 11

Nurturing the Seeds of Innovation: Brainstorming and Ideation 11

Identifying Market Gaps and Opportunities: Seeds of Impact 12

Personal Testimony: A Seed of Innovation 14

In Conclusion 14

Chapter 4: Idea Validation 16

Cultivating Sustainable Growth: Market Research and Competitive Analysis 16

Personal Testimony: The Growth of an Idea ... 18

In Conclusion 19

Part 3: Building Your Business Plan 20

Chapter 5: Crafting a Solid Business Plan .. 21

Laying the Foundation: A Strategic Business Plan 21

Defining Your Audience and Value Proposition: Building on a Solid Rock 22

Personal Testimony: A Mission-Driven Plan .. 24

In Conclusion 24

Chapter 6: Market Strategy and Positioning 26

Navigating the Marketplace: Crafting a Winning Strategy 26

Establishing a Unique Brand Identity and Market Position 27

Personal Testimony: A Brand with Purpose ... 28

In Conclusion 29

Part 4: Legal and Financial Foundations ... 30

Chapter 7: Legal Considerations 31

Building on Solid Ground: Choosing the Right Legal Structure 31

Navigating Licenses, Permits, and Intellectual Property: A Solid Framework 32

Personal Testimony: A Foundation of Compliance 33

In Conclusion 34

Chapter 8: Financial Planning and Funding 35

    Building a Strong Financial Framework: Realistic Projections 35

    Exploring Funding Options: A Strong Pillar of Support 36

    Personal Testimony: The Path to Financial Stability 37

    In Conclusion 38

Part 5: Launching Your Business 39

Chapter 9: Pre-Launch Preparation 40

    Setting the Stage: Building a Strong Online Presence 40

    Developing a Pre-Launch Marketing and Buzz Strategy: Building Excitement 41

    Personal Testimony: Igniting the Pre-Launch Buzz 42

    In Conclusion 43

Chapter 10: Launch Day and Beyond 44

    Embarking on the Journey: Executing a Successful Launch 44

Continuously Refining Your Product: Navigating the Ongoing Journey 45

Personal Testimony: A Journey of Growth 46

In Conclusion 47

Part 6: Growing and Scaling 48

Chapter 11: Scaling Strategies 49

Reaching New Horizons: Strategies for Successful Scaling 49

Expanding Your Reach: Product Line, Customer Base, and Beyond 50

Personal Testimony: Navigating the Heights .. 51

In Conclusion 52

Chapter 12: Managing Operations and Teams 53

Sailing Smooth Waters: Efficiently Managing Operations 53

Building and Leading High-Performing Teams: A Unity of Purpose 54

Personal Testimony: Guiding the Ship 55

In Conclusion 56

Part 7: Navigating Challenges 57

Chapter 13: Overcoming Entrepreneurial Challenges..58

Climbing Mountains: Rising Above Entrepreneurial Challenges............................58

Managing Stress and Maintaining Work-Life Balance: Nurturing the Self............................59

Personal Testimony: Climbing the Peaks 60

In Conclusion 61

Chapter 14: Sustaining Long-Term Success 62

Planting Seeds of Endurance: Adapting and Evolving 62

Evolving Your Business: Nurturing Growth and Competitiveness..63

Personal Testimony: Navigating Change........64

In Conclusion 65

Part 8: Exit Strategies and Legacy 66

Chapter 15: Exit Planning 67

Closing One Chapter, Opening Another: Exploring Exit Strategies 67

Preparing Your Business for a Successful Exit: Ensuring Continuity 68

Personal Testimony: Closing One Chapter, Opening Another 69

In Conclusion 70

Chapter 16: Leaving a Lasting Impact 71

Planting Seeds of Legacy: Creating a Positive Impact 71

Mentoring the Next Generation: Passing the Torch 72

Personal Testimony: Sowing Seeds of Impact 73

In Conclusion 74

Appendices: 75

A. Resources for Further Reading, Tools, and Templates 75

B. Case Studies of Successful Startups and Their Journeys 88

C. Glossary of Entrepreneurship and Business Terms 98

Part 1:

The Entrepreneurial Mindset

Chapter 1:

Introduction to Entrepreneurship

Entrepreneurship: A Journey of Creation and Innovation

At its core, entrepreneurship is the journey of creation and innovation. It's about identifying unmet needs, crafting solutions, and bringing those solutions to life in the form of products, services, or experiences. This journey requires a combination of creativity, determination, and a willingness to embrace uncertainty. Just as the Creator formed the world from chaos, entrepreneurs shape new realities out of uncharted territories.

*"In the beginning, God created the heavens and the earth." - **Genesis 1:1***

Overcoming Myths and Misconceptions

Myth: Entrepreneurship is Only for the Wealthy

Reality: Entrepreneurship is not limited by financial status. Many successful businesses were born from humble beginnings. For instance, the story of Steve Jobs and Steve Wozniak starting Apple Computer in a garage emphasizes how innovation and dedication supersede initial resources.

Myth: Entrepreneurs Are Risk-Takers

Reality: While entrepreneurship involves risk, calculated decisions backed by research and strategy are more common than reckless gambles. Noah's decision to build the ark despite societal skepticism and impending challenges showcases how faith in one's vision can lead to success.

"By faith Noah, when warned about things not yet seen, in holy fear built an ark to save his family." - **Hebrews 11:7**

Myth: Success Happens Overnight

Reality: Entrepreneurial success often requires years of hard work, learning, and refinement. Just as Joseph's journey from slavery to prominence in Egypt spanned many trials, entrepreneurial journeys are marked by persistence and resilience.

"The Lord was with Joseph and he prospered, and he lived in the house of his Egyptian master." - **Genesis 39:2**

Myth: Entrepreneurship is Lonely

Reality: Collaboration and networking play vital roles in entrepreneurship. Even Jesus surrounded himself with disciples to spread his message. Building a team and seeking mentorship can provide valuable support on the entrepreneurial path.

*"Come, follow me," Jesus said, "and I will send you out to fish for people." - **Matthew 4:19***

Conclusion

In this chapter, we've introduced the essence of entrepreneurship as a journey of creation and innovation. By dispelling common myths, we've paved the way for a deeper exploration of the entrepreneurial mindset. Just as biblical figures overcame challenges and believed in their visions, so too can modern entrepreneurs shape their destinies. In the upcoming chapters, we'll delve into the mindset traits necessary for success, allowing you to harness your potential and create a lasting impact through entrepreneurship.

Chapter 2:

Cultivating the Entrepreneurial Mindset

Developing an Entrepreneurial Mindset: Seeds of Success

The entrepreneurial journey is not only about business strategies but also about nurturing a mindset that fosters success. Cultivating this mindset involves developing key traits that empower entrepreneurs to thrive in the face of challenges and uncertainty.

"For as he thinks in his heart, so is he." - **Proverbs 23:7**

1. **Creativity:** Just as God's creativity knows no bounds in shaping the universe, entrepreneurs

must tap into their creative wellsprings to innovate. Consider the story of Thomas Edison, who, through countless iterations, invented the practical light bulb. Creative thinking transforms obstacles into opportunities.

2. **Resilience:** The biblical story of Job exemplifies resilience in the face of adversity. Similarly, entrepreneurs must withstand setbacks, using challenges as stepping stones to growth. Adversity strengthens character and prepares entrepreneurs for greater achievements.

*"I know the plans I have for you, plans to prosper you and not to harm you, plans to give you hope and a future." - **Jeremiah 29:11***

3. **Adaptability:** The ability to adapt is key in both biblical narratives and entrepreneurship. Consider the journey of the Israelites in the desert—adaptive thinking ensured their survival. Entrepreneurs must navigate shifting landscapes by being open to change and evolving their strategies.

Navigating Risk and Uncertainty with Faith

Entrepreneurship is inherently marked by risk and uncertainty, much like the faith journey portrayed in the Bible. Just as Abraham embarked on a journey to an unknown land with unwavering faith, entrepreneurs must approach risk with courage and belief in their visions.

"By faith Abraham, when called to go to a place he would later receive as his inheritance, obeyed and went, even though he did not know where he was going." - **Hebrews 11:8**

1. **Positive Outlook:** Facing risk requires a positive outlook. Like David, who approached Goliath with confidence, entrepreneurs should embrace challenges as opportunities for growth. A positive perspective fuels resilience and propels entrepreneurs forward.

> *"The Lord who delivered me from the paw of the lion and the paw of the bear will deliver me from the hand of this Philistine."* - **1 Samuel 17:37**

Personal Testimony: Navigating Stormy Seas

I, too, have experienced the transformative power of an entrepreneurial mindset. When I started my own business, I faced numerous obstacles that tested my determination. There were moments when doubt and uncertainty threatened to overpower me. However, by embracing creativity, resilience, and adaptability, I navigated those stormy seas. Through faith and a positive outlook, I transformed challenges into stepping stones. Just as the disciples' faith was tested on a stormy sea, my faith in my vision carried me through, ultimately leading to the success of my venture.

In Conclusion

Cultivating the entrepreneurial mindset involves developing creativity, resilience, and adaptability while facing risk and uncertainty with faith and positivity. By drawing inspiration from biblical stories of faith and perseverance, entrepreneurs can harness the power of their mindset to shape their journey toward success. The seeds of the entrepreneurial mindset, once planted and nurtured, can yield a bountiful harvest of innovation and achievement.

Part 2:
Ideation and Validation

Chapter 3:

Generating Business Ideas

Nurturing the Seeds of Innovation: Brainstorming and Ideation

Entrepreneurship often begins with a spark of inspiration, a creative idea that has the potential to blossom into a successful business. Just as God's creation was born from divine inspiration, entrepreneurs can harness techniques for brainstorming and ideation to generate innovative concepts.

"He has filled them with skill to do all kinds of work as engravers, designers, embroiderers in blue, purple and scarlet yarn and fine linen, and weavers—all of them skilled workers and designers." - ***Exodus 35:35***

1. **Mind Mapping:** Like the intricate design of the Tabernacle, mind mapping involves creating visual representations of ideas. Start with a central concept and branch out, exploring related ideas. This technique encourages connections and sparks fresh insights.

2. **Role Reversal:** In the story of the Good Samaritan, a compassionate act stemmed from a different perspective. Entrepreneurs can adopt this approach by imagining themselves in different roles, leading to ideas that address diverse needs.

Identifying Market Gaps and Opportunities: Seeds of Impact

Biblical narratives often highlight the importance of recognizing needs and opportunities. Just as Nehemiah saw the broken walls of Jerusalem and took action, entrepreneurs must identify market gaps to create meaningful solutions.

"I also said to the king, 'If it pleases the king, may I have letters to the governors of Trans-Euphrates, so that they will provide me safe-conduct until I arrive in Judah? And may I have a letter to Asaph, keeper of the royal park, so he will give me timber to make beams for the gates of the citadel by the temple and for the city wall and for the residence I will occupy?'" - **Nehemiah 2:7-8**

1. **Observation:** Just as Jesus observed the needs of the hungry crowd and multiplied the loaves and fishes, entrepreneurs can keenly observe their surroundings. Identifying unmet needs or pain points can lead to innovative solutions.

2. **Customer Empathy:** The story of the woman with the issue of blood showcases empathy. Entrepreneurs must empathize with their target audience to understand their challenges deeply. Solutions born from empathy are often the most impactful.

Personal Testimony: A Seed of Innovation

When I set out to start my own business, I faced a dilemma: finding a unique offering in a saturated market. Through mind mapping, I explored various angles and discovered a niche that no one else had tapped into. This approach led me to develop a product that addressed an unmet need, and my business flourished as a result. Just as biblical characters identified opportunities to make a difference, my journey was marked by finding the right market gap and seizing it with creativity and determination.

In Conclusion

Generating business ideas is akin to planting seeds of innovation. By employing techniques like mind mapping and role reversal, entrepreneurs can nurture the growth of their ideas. Recognizing market gaps and opportunities requires observation and customer empathy, leading to solutions that create meaningful impact. Just as seeds planted in fertile soil yield bountiful harvests, entrepreneurial ideas nurtured with creativity and market insight can flourish into successful ventures.

Chapter 4:

Idea Validation

Cultivating Sustainable Growth: Market Research and Competitive Analysis

Just as a farmer assesses the conditions of the soil before planting seeds, entrepreneurs must diligently conduct market research and competitive analysis to ensure the viability of their business ideas. By taking these steps, they can sow the seeds of success with confidence.

"For which of you, intending to build a tower, does not sit down first and count the cost, whether he has enough to finish it?" - ***Luke 14:28***

1. **Market Research:** Like the wise men who followed the star to find the newborn Jesus, entrepreneurs must follow the signs of market

demand. By researching demographics, trends, and consumer behaviors, they can tailor their offerings to meet genuine needs.

2. **Competitive Analysis:** In the parable of the talents, the servant who invested wisely multiplied his resources. Similarly, entrepreneurs should analyze their competitors to understand their strengths and weaknesses. This knowledge enables entrepreneurs to position their offerings effectively.

Cultivating Fertile Ground: Creating a Minimum Viable Product (MVP)

Just as a gardener nurtures a young plant, entrepreneurs must nurture their business ideas through practical testing. Creating a Minimum Viable Product (MVP) is like planting a seedling, allowing entrepreneurs to gather valuable feedback and refine their concept before full-scale implementation.

"Like newborn babies, crave pure spiritual milk, so that by it you may grow up in your salvation." - 1 Peter 2:2

1. **Building a Prototype:** Just as God created humans in his image, entrepreneurs give form to their ideas through prototypes. MVPs are stripped-down versions of the final product, providing a tangible representation that can be tested and refined.

2. **Gathering Feedback:** As Jesus sought the opinions of his disciples, entrepreneurs should seek feedback from potential customers. This input helps identify areas for improvement and ensures that the final product aligns with market needs.

Personal Testimony: The Growth of an Idea

In my own entrepreneurial journey, I envisioned a product that aimed to simplify a common daily task. Through rigorous market research and competitive analysis, I understood the nuances of consumer preferences and identified key differentiators. By creating an MVP and gathering feedback, I fine-tuned my product's features and user experience. This process allowed my idea to grow from a mere concept into a viable, user-centric solution. Just as the nurturing of a young plant yields a bountiful harvest, nurturing an MVP paves the way for a successful business venture.

In Conclusion

Idea validation is the process of nurturing the seeds of innovation by conducting thorough market research, competitive analysis, and creating a Minimum Viable Product (MVP). Just as a farmer tends to the soil before planting, entrepreneurs must cultivate a solid foundation for their ideas. Through these steps, they can ensure that their concepts align with market demands and possess the potential for sustainable growth. With an attentive approach to validation, entrepreneurs lay the groundwork for a thriving venture that can weather the challenges ahead.

Part 3:

Building Your Business Plan

Chapter 5:
Crafting a Solid Business Plan

Laying the Foundation: A Strategic Business Plan

Much like a master architect designs a blueprint, entrepreneurs craft a business plan to outline the structure and direction of their ventures. This chapter focuses on the critical elements of a business plan—laying the groundwork for a successful journey.

"Suppose one of you wants to build a tower. Won't you first sit down and estimate the cost to see if you have enough money to complete it?" - **Luke 14:28**

1. **Executive Summary:** Just as a psalm encapsulates the essence of a message, the

executive summary encapsulates the core of the business plan. It concisely introduces the business, its goals, and its value proposition.

2. **Mission and Vision:** Like the mission of Christ, a business's mission guides its purpose and direction. The vision paints a picture of where the business is headed. Entrepreneurs must align their goals with a higher purpose, just as Jesus did when he shared his mission.

> *"The Spirit of the Lord is on me, because he has anointed me to proclaim good news to the poor." -* **Luke 4:18**

Defining Your Audience and Value Proposition: Building on a Solid Rock

In the parable of the wise and foolish builders, Jesus emphasized the importance of a strong foundation. Similarly, entrepreneurs must lay a strong foundation by identifying their target audience and crafting a compelling value proposition.

"Therefore everyone who hears these words of mine and puts them into practice is like a wise man who built his house on the rock." - **Matthew 7:24**

1. **Target Audience:** Just as Jesus tailored his teachings to various audiences, entrepreneurs must understand the demographics, needs, and preferences of their target market. This knowledge helps create products and experiences that resonate deeply.

2. **Value Proposition:** Jesus offered the ultimate value proposition—eternal salvation. Similarly, entrepreneurs must clearly communicate the unique value their products or services offer to customers. This differentiation is what sets them apart in a crowded marketplace.

Personal Testimony: A Mission-Driven Plan

In my entrepreneurial journey, I felt a calling to create a business that not only generated profit but also contributed to environmental sustainability. Crafting a business plan that aligned with this mission allowed me to attract investors and customers who shared the same values. Just as Jesus's mission resonated with those seeking spiritual growth, a mission-driven plan resonates with customers seeking purposeful products and experiences.

In Conclusion

Crafting a solid business plan is akin to building a foundation upon which a successful venture can flourish. By structuring the plan with essential elements like the executive summary, mission, vision, goals, target audience, and value proposition, entrepreneurs set the stage for their journey. Just as a solid rock provides stability, a well-crafted business plan provides direction and purpose, guiding entrepreneurs toward their desired destination of success.

Chapter 6:

Market Strategy and Positioning

Navigating the Marketplace: Crafting a Winning Strategy

Just as a skilled navigator charts a course through uncharted waters, entrepreneurs must develop a comprehensive marketing strategy to guide their business through the competitive marketplace. This chapter delves into the art of strategic marketing and establishing a unique brand identity.

*"For which of you, intending to build a tower, does not sit down first and count the cost, whether he has enough to finish it ?" - **Luke 14:28***

1. **Comprehensive Marketing Strategy:** Like a general planning a battle, entrepreneurs must analyze their strengths, weaknesses, opportunities, and threats. Through this SWOT analysis, they can develop a strategy that highlights strengths, mitigates weaknesses, capitalizes on opportunities, and defends against threats.

2. **Market Segmentation:** Just as Jesus tailored his teachings to various audiences, entrepreneurs must segment their target market based on demographics, psychographics, and behaviors. This allows for personalized messaging that resonates with each segment.

Establishing a Unique Brand Identity and Market Position

The story of the Good Shepherd highlights the importance of differentiation and nurturing a unique identity. Similarly, entrepreneurs must carefully craft their brand identity and position themselves distinctively in the market.

"I am the good shepherd. The good shepherd lays down his life for the sheep." - **John 10:11**

1. **Brand Identity:** Just as Jesus's teachings reflected his core values, a brand's identity reflects its essence. Entrepreneurs must define their brand's personality, values, and attributes. A well-defined brand identity forms the foundation of customer relationships.

2. **Market Positioning:** In a crowded marketplace, positioning is key. Entrepreneurs must decide where their product or service fits within the market landscape. Are they the luxury option, the affordable choice, or the innovative disruptor? This decision shapes customer perceptions.

Personal Testimony: A Brand with Purpose

In my own entrepreneurial journey, I recognized the power of aligning my brand with a meaningful purpose. By crafting a brand identity rooted in sustainability and social responsibility, I not only attracted customers who shared these values but also fostered a sense of loyalty and community. Just as Jesus's identity as the Good Shepherd resonated with those seeking guidance, a purpose-driven brand identity resonates with customers seeking alignment with their values.

In Conclusion

Crafting a comprehensive marketing strategy and establishing a unique brand identity are essential steps in the entrepreneurial journey. Just as a navigator sets sail with a clear plan, entrepreneurs must guide their business through the marketplace with a well-defined strategy. By understanding their market, segmenting their audience, and differentiating themselves through brand identity and positioning, entrepreneurs create a strong presence that resonates with customers and sets the stage for success.

Part 4:
Legal and Financial Foundations

Chapter 7:

Legal Considerations

Building on Solid Ground: Choosing the Right Legal Structure

Just as a builder selects the right foundation for a structure, entrepreneurs must choose the appropriate legal structure for their business. This chapter delves into the importance of legal considerations and the impact of selecting the right structure.

"Suppose one of you wants to build a tower. Won't you first sit down and estimate the cost to see if you have enough money to complete it?" - **Luke 14:28**

1. **Legal Structure Options:** Like the various building materials available, entrepreneurs have multiple legal structures to choose from, including sole proprietorships, partnerships, LLCs, and corporations. Each structure has unique implications for liability, taxation, and management.

2. **Liability Protection:** Just as homeowners protect themselves with insurance, entrepreneurs shield themselves from personal liability by selecting the appropriate legal structure. A well-chosen structure can safeguard personal assets from business-related liabilities.

Navigating Licenses, Permits, and Intellectual Property: A Solid Framework

In the parable of the wise and foolish builders, Jesus emphasized the importance of a strong foundation. Similarly, entrepreneurs must establish a solid framework by understanding and securing the necessary licenses, permits, and intellectual property rights.

*"Therefore everyone who hears these words of mine and puts them into practice is like a wise man who built his house on the rock." - **Matthew 7:24***

1. **Licenses and Permits:** Just as a homeowner needs permits for construction, entrepreneurs must navigate licenses and permits required by local, state, and federal authorities. This ensures compliance and prevents legal complications down the road.

2. **Intellectual Property Protection:** Like creators seeking copyright protection, entrepreneurs must safeguard their intellectual property, such as trademarks, patents, and copyrights. This protection preserves the uniqueness of their creations and prevents unauthorized use.

Personal Testimony: A Foundation of Compliance

In my entrepreneurial journey, I recognized the significance of legal compliance early on. By carefully selecting the right legal structure and obtaining the necessary licenses, I established a solid foundation for growth. This decision not only protected my personal assets but also facilitated smooth operations as I expanded my business. Just as building on solid ground ensures stability, a foundation of legal compliance provides entrepreneurs the confidence to focus on their goals.

In Conclusion

Legal considerations serve as the foundation upon which entrepreneurs build their ventures. By choosing the right legal structure, navigating licenses and permits, and safeguarding intellectual property, entrepreneurs ensure that their business is built on solid ground. Just as a well-constructed structure withstands the test of time, a business built with legal and financial foresight is poised for long-term success and growth.

Chapter 8:

Financial Planning and Funding

Building a Strong Financial Framework: Realistic Projections

Just as a builder relies on architectural plans, entrepreneurs depend on realistic financial projections to guide their business. This chapter emphasizes the importance of financial planning and projecting a stable future.

"For which of you, intending to build a tower, does not sit down first and count the cost, whether he has enough to finish it?" - **Luke 14:28**

1. **Financial Projections:** Like an architect sketches out a building's dimensions, entrepreneurs must outline their financial expectations. Realistic

projections help assess revenue, expenses, and potential profitability over a defined period.

2. **Budgeting:** In the story of Joseph's prudent management during famine, budgeting plays a crucial role. Entrepreneurs must allocate resources wisely, allowing for contingencies and ensuring financial stability.

Exploring Funding Options: A Strong Pillar of Support

Just as a builder secures strong pillars for stability, entrepreneurs must explore various funding options to support their business. This chapter delves into the importance of funding and different avenues entrepreneurs can explore.

"Suppose one of you wants to build a tower. Won't you first sit down and estimate the cost to see if you have enough money to complete it?" - **Luke 14:28**

1. **Bootstrapping:** Like the widow's oil that never ran out, entrepreneurs can start small and gradually reinvest profits into their business. Bootstrapping fosters financial independence and minimizes debt.

2. **Investors:** Just as the parable of the talents features wise investment, entrepreneurs can seek investors who believe in their vision. Investors provide capital in exchange for equity or ownership stakes, allowing entrepreneurs to scale faster.

3. **Loans and Financing:** The biblical concept of sowing and reaping applies to financing as well. Entrepreneurs can secure loans from banks, credit unions, or online lenders to bridge financial gaps and fuel growth.

Personal Testimony: The Path to Financial Stability

In my own journey, I realized the significance of detailed financial projections and prudent funding choices. By meticulously projecting revenues and expenses, I gained a clearer picture of my business's financial health. Additionally, exploring funding options—like bootstrapping in the early stages and later securing strategic investors—provided me with a solid financial pillar to build upon. Just as biblical wisdom guided Joseph to manage resources during challenging times, strategic financial planning guided my business through both lean and prosperous periods.

In Conclusion

Financial planning and funding are integral pillars of a successful business. By creating realistic financial projections and exploring various funding options, entrepreneurs build a strong foundation for growth. Just as a builder constructs a sturdy structure with dependable pillars, entrepreneurs create a financially sound business poised for stability and resilience.

Part 5:
Launching Your Business

Chapter 9:

Pre-Launch Preparation

Setting the Stage: Building a Strong Online Presence

Just as a playwright sets the stage before a performance, entrepreneurs must establish a robust online presence to create anticipation for their business launch. This chapter emphasizes the importance of online visibility and preparation.

"For which of you, intending to build a tower, does not sit down first and count the cost, whether he has enough to finish it?" - **Luke 14:28**

1. **Website Development:** Like constructing a theater for a grand play, entrepreneurs must create a polished and functional website. A user-friendly

website is a vital hub for information, interaction, and transactions with customers.

2. **Content Creation:** Much like a playwright crafts compelling dialogues, entrepreneurs must create engaging and informative content. Blogs, videos, and social media posts help generate interest, establish expertise, and create a community.

Developing a Pre-Launch Marketing and Buzz Strategy: Building Excitement

In the parable of the sower, the seeds that fall on fertile soil yield bountiful harvests. Similarly, entrepreneurs must sow the seeds of anticipation by developing a pre-launch marketing and buzz strategy.

"A farmer went out to sow his seed. As he was scattering the seed, some fell along the path, and the birds came and ate it up." - **Luke 8:5**

1. **Social Media Teasers:** Just as the anticipation of a dramatic climax keeps the audience engaged, entrepreneurs can release teaser content on social media platforms. Sneak peeks, behind-the-scenes insights, and countdowns build excitement.

2. **Email Campaigns:** In the story of the prodigal son's return, celebration ensued. Similarly, entrepreneurs can invite their audience to a *"launch celebration"* by sending email campaigns that highlight the upcoming launch and its value.

Personal Testimony: Igniting the Pre-Launch Buzz

In my own entrepreneurial journey, I recognized the power of a strong online presence and pre-launch marketing. By developing an informative and user-friendly website, I created a central hub for customers to explore my offerings. Additionally, crafting teaser content and engaging in social media campaigns generated buzz and excitement before my business launch. Just as the anticipation of a grand performance fuels excitement, the pre-launch buzz I cultivated heightened interest and laid the foundation for a successful launch.

In Conclusion

Pre-launch preparation is akin to setting the stage for a captivating performance. By building a strong online presence, creating engaging content, and developing a pre-launch marketing strategy, entrepreneurs create anticipation and excitement among their target audience. Just as a well-prepared stage enhances the impact of a play, effective pre-launch strategies enhance the impact of a business launch, setting the tone for a successful journey ahead.

Chapter 10:

Launch Day and Beyond

Embarking on the Journey: Executing a Successful Launch

Just as a ship sets sail on its maiden voyage, entrepreneurs must execute a meticulously planned launch to propel their business into the market. This chapter emphasizes the importance of launch execution and the journey that follows.

*"For which of you, intending to build a tower, does not sit down first and count the cost, whether he has enough to finish it?" - **Luke 14:28***

1. **Launch Plan Execution:** Like a captain guiding a ship, entrepreneurs must execute their

launch plan with precision. This involves coordinated efforts across marketing, sales, customer service, and operations to ensure a smooth introduction to the market.

2. **Customer Engagement:** Just as a ship's journey relies on favorable winds, entrepreneurs must engage their customers post-launch. Feedback, reviews, and interactions allow entrepreneurs to understand customer reactions, make improvements, and build loyalty.

Continuously Refining Your Product: Navigating the Ongoing Journey

In the parable of the mustard seed, a small seed grows into a large tree. Similarly, entrepreneurs must nurture their business by continuously refining their product based on feedback and insights.

"He told them another parable: 'The kingdom of heaven is like a mustard seed, which a man took and planted in his field.'" - **Matthew 13:31**

1. **Feedback Collection:** Just as a farmer tends to crops, entrepreneurs must tend to their product by collecting customer feedback. This feedback provides valuable insights into areas for improvement, potential features, and emerging trends.

2. **Iterative Development:** In the story of the persistent widow, perseverance pays off. Similarly, entrepreneurs must persistently refine their product based on feedback. Iterative development ensures that the product evolves to meet changing customer needs.

Personal Testimony: A Journey of Growth

In my entrepreneurial journey, the launch day marked a significant milestone, but the journey didn't end there. By executing a well-planned launch, I introduced my product to the market *with impact. However, the real growth came from continuously engaging with customers, gathering feedback, and refining the product. Just as a journey unfolds with each step taken, my business grew through ongoing improvement and adaptation based on customer insights.*

In Conclusion

Launching a business is a pivotal moment, but the journey continues beyond that day. By executing a successful launch plan, entrepreneurs introduce their offerings to the market with impact. However, the ongoing journey involves engaging customers, gathering feedback, and iteratively refining the product to meet evolving needs. Just as a ship's voyage leads to uncharted waters, an entrepreneur's journey leads to innovation, growth, and lasting success.

Part 6:

Growing and Scaling

Chapter 11:

Scaling Strategies

Reaching New Horizons: Strategies for Successful Scaling

Just as a plant reaches for the sun, entrepreneurs must reach for new heights through strategic scaling. This chapter delves into the art of scaling a business while maintaining quality and expanding reach.

"For which of you, intending to build a tower, does not sit down first and count the cost, whether he has enough to finish it?" - **Luke 14:28**

1. **Strategic Scaling:** Like a pilot navigating the skies, entrepreneurs must adopt strategies for rapid growth. These include replicating successful processes, optimizing operations, and leveraging technology to handle increased demand.

2. **Maintaining Quality:** In the story of the feeding of the five thousand, quality was not compromised despite the scale. Similarly, entrepreneurs must ensure that as they grow, the quality of their products, services, and customer experiences remains consistent.

Expanding Your Reach: Product Line, Customer Base, and Beyond

Just as a tree grows branches to reach new heights, entrepreneurs must expand their business's reach by diversifying their product offerings, reaching a wider customer base, and exploring new geographic markets.

"He told them another parable: 'The kingdom of heaven is like a mustard seed, which a man took and planted in his field.'" - **Matthew 13:31**

1. **Diversification:** Just as a farmer diversifies crops, entrepreneurs can expand their product line to cater to different customer needs. Offering complementary products or services enhances the overall customer experience.

2. **Reaching a Wider Audience:** The story of the prodigal son's return illustrates the impact of reaching a broader audience. Entrepreneurs can use targeted marketing and strategic partnerships to reach new customer segments.

Personal Testimony: Navigating the Heights

In my journey of scaling, I realized the importance of maintaining a delicate balance. By adopting strategic scaling strategies and diversifying my product line, I successfully expanded my business's reach. However, I learned that maintaining quality and consistent customer experiences at every touchpoint was paramount. Just as scaling a mountain requires careful steps, scaling a business demands mindful strategies that ensure growth while safeguarding the core values that drove its success.

In Conclusion

Scaling a business is a remarkable phase that requires strategic planning and careful execution. By adopting growth strategies while preserving quality, entrepreneurs can reach new heights without compromising their business's essence. Just as a tree's branches extend to new horizons, scaling strategies allow entrepreneurs to diversify their offerings, attract a broader audience, and expand their impact across geographic regions. Through mindful growth, entrepreneurs lay the foundation for a lasting legacy of success.

Chapter 12:

Managing Operations and Teams

Sailing Smooth Waters: Efficiently Managing Operations

Just as a skilled captain navigates a ship through calm waters, entrepreneurs must efficiently manage resources and operations to keep their business sailing smoothly. This chapter focuses on effective operations management for sustained success.

"For which of you, intending to build a tower, does not sit down first and count the cost, whether he has enough to finish it?" - **Luke 14:28**

1. **Resource Allocation:** Like a wise steward managing resources, entrepreneurs must allocate

funds, time, and personnel effectively. Prioritizing projects and streamlining processes prevents wastage and maximizes efficiency.

2. **Operational Processes:** In the story of the loaves and fishes, Jesus organized the distribution efficiently. Similarly, entrepreneurs must establish clear operational processes that ensure consistent quality, timely delivery, and customer satisfaction.

Building and Leading High-Performing Teams: A Unity of Purpose

Just as a skilled conductor leads an orchestra, entrepreneurs must build and lead high-performing teams that work harmoniously towards a common goal. This chapter delves into the art of team management.

*"Now you are the body of Christ, and each one of you is a part of it." - **1 Corinthians 12:27***

1. **Team Building:** Like Jesus assembling his disciples, entrepreneurs must carefully select team members who align with the business's values and vision. A diverse team with complementary skills fosters creativity and problem-solving.

2. **Leadership:** Just as Jesus led his disciples with humility, entrepreneurs must lead with empathy and inspiration. Effective leadership involves setting clear expectations, providing guidance, and recognizing and nurturing talent.

Personal Testimony: Guiding the Ship

In my journey of managing operations and teams, I realized the significance of fostering a unified purpose and efficient practices. By allocating resources wisely and refining operational processes, I created a solid foundation for my business's growth. Additionally, assembling a dedicated and skilled team allowed me to delegate responsibilities and leverage diverse expertise.

Just as a ship's captain guides the vessel through calm and stormy seas, effective operations management and team leadership guide a business towards success in various conditions.

In Conclusion

Efficiently managing operations and leading high-performing teams are essential aspects of running a successful business. By allocating resources effectively, streamlining processes, and fostering a cohesive team, entrepreneurs ensure their business operates smoothly. Just as a skilled conductor leads a symphony to produce harmonious music, effective team leadership orchestrates collaborative efforts that lead to impressive outcomes. Through sound operations and strong team dynamics, entrepreneurs set the stage for continued growth and prosperity.

Part 7:
Navigating Challenges

Chapter 13:

Overcoming Entrepreneurial Challenges

Climbing Mountains: Rising Above Entrepreneurial Challenges

Just as climbers face obstacles on their ascent, entrepreneurs encounter challenges on their journey. This chapter delves into overcoming failure, setbacks, and maintaining well-being while navigating the entrepreneurial path.

"For which of you, intending to build a tower, does not sit down first and count the cost, whether he has enough to finish it?" - **Luke 14:28**

1. **Embracing Failure and Setbacks:** Like a climber who learns from each slip, entrepreneurs must embrace failure as a stepping stone to success. By learning from mistakes and setbacks, they gain valuable insights that lead to growth.

2. **Pivoting and Adaptation:** In the story of Paul's conversion, adaptation played a significant role. Similarly, entrepreneurs must be open to pivoting their strategies and adapting to changing market conditions, ensuring they stay relevant and resilient.

Managing Stress and Maintaining Work-Life Balance: Nurturing the Self

Just as a well-nourished body performs better, entrepreneurs must nurture their mental and emotional well-being to navigate challenges effectively. This chapter emphasizes the importance of stress management and work-life balance.

*"Come to me, all you who are weary and burdened, and I will give you rest." - **Matthew 11:28***

1. **Stress Management:** Just as Jesus offered rest to the weary, entrepreneurs must prioritize self-care. Techniques like meditation, exercise, and time management help manage stress and maintain mental clarity during challenging times.

2. **Work-Life Balance:** The story of the Sabbath emphasizes rest and rejuvenation. Entrepreneurs must strike a balance between work and personal life to prevent burnout and foster long-term sustainability.

Personal Testimony: Climbing the Peaks

In my entrepreneurial journey, I encountered my share of challenges and setbacks. By reframing failures as learning opportunities and staying open to adapting my strategies, I transformed challenges into stepping stones towards growth.

Additionally, nurturing my well-being through stress management and maintaining a work-life balance allowed me to navigate rough patches with resilience. Just as a climber ascends a challenging peak, I embraced challenges as part of the journey, utilizing them to propel myself higher.

In Conclusion

Overcoming entrepreneurial challenges is an inherent part of the journey. By embracing failures, setbacks, and adapting strategies, entrepreneurs learn and grow stronger. Prioritizing stress management and work-life balance ensures that entrepreneurs navigate challenges with a clear mind and sustained energy. Just as climbers conquer mountains with determination and careful preparation, entrepreneurs overcome challenges by harnessing their resilience, adaptability, and well-being. Through these efforts, entrepreneurs not only conquer obstacles but also lay the foundation for enduring success.

Chapter 14:

Sustaining Long-Term Success

Planting Seeds of Endurance: Adapting and Evolving

Just as a farmer adapts to changing seasons, entrepreneurs must adapt to market changes and trends to sustain long-term success. This chapter focuses on the art of evolving a business to remain competitive.

"For which of you, intending to build a tower, does not sit down first and count the cost, whether he has enough to finish it?" - **Luke 14:28**

1. **Market Sensitivity:** Like a farmer who monitors weather patterns, entrepreneurs must stay attuned to market changes and emerging trends. This awareness helps them identify shifts in

customer preferences and pivot their strategies accordingly.

2. **Continuous Innovation:** In the story of the talents, the servant who multiplied his resources demonstrated initiative and creativity. Similarly, entrepreneurs must embrace innovation and evolve their offerings to meet new demands and stay relevant.

Evolving Your Business: Nurturing Growth and Competitiveness

Just as a plant evolves to adapt to its environment, entrepreneurs must evolve their business to thrive in a dynamic market. This involves embracing change and actively seeking growth opportunities.

"But grow in the grace and knowledge of our Lord and Savior Jesus Christ." - **2 Peter 3:18**

1. **Diversification:** Like the Apostle Paul adapting his message to different audiences, entrepreneurs can diversify their business offerings. Expanding product lines, entering new markets, or providing additional services enhances the business's reach and relevance.

2. **Collaborative Partnerships:** Just as Jesus collaborated with disciples to achieve his mission, entrepreneurs can collaborate with partners to expand their reach and capabilities. Joint ventures, strategic alliances, and partnerships can open doors to new opportunities.

Personal Testimony: Navigating Change

In my journey of sustaining long-term success, I realized the importance of embracing change and actively evolving. By staying attuned to market shifts and customer preferences, I was able to pivot my strategies and offerings to remain competitive. Additionally, fostering a culture of continuous innovation within my team allowed us to adapt quickly and stay ahead of trends. Just as a plant adapts to its environment to flourish, my business evolved to thrive amidst changing dynamics, ultimately ensuring enduring success.

In Conclusion

Sustaining long-term success requires a commitment to adaptation and evolution. By staying sensitive to market changes, embracing innovation, and actively evolving offerings, entrepreneurs ensure that their business remains competitive and relevant. Just as plants adapt to changing conditions to flourish, entrepreneurs nurture growth and competitiveness by proactively adapting to the evolving landscape. Through these efforts, entrepreneurs lay the groundwork for a legacy of enduring success and impact.

Part 8:
Exit Strategies and Legacy

Chapter 15:

Exit Planning

Closing One Chapter, Opening Another: Exploring Exit Strategies

Just as a book concludes with an ending, entrepreneurs must plan for the eventual conclusion of their business journey. This chapter delves into exit planning, exploring options like acquisition, merger, or IPO, and preparing for a successful transition.

"For which of you, intending to build a tower, does not sit down first and count the cost, whether he has enough to finish it?" - **Luke 14:28**

1. **Exit Strategy Options:** Like a traveler planning their next destination, entrepreneurs must explore various exit options. These include selling the business through acquisition, merging with another company, or taking the business public through an Initial Public Offering (IPO).

2. **Financial Preparedness:** Just as a prudent builder saves for the future, entrepreneurs must ensure their business's financial stability and profitability before considering an exit. A healthy balance sheet and sustainable revenue streams increase the business's attractiveness to potential buyers or investors.

Preparing Your Business for a Successful Exit: Ensuring Continuity

In the story of Joseph, his preparation during times of abundance helped sustain his family during famine. Similarly, entrepreneurs must prepare their business for a successful exit to ensure its continuity and prosperity under new ownership.

*"So when Joseph came to his brothers, they stripped him of his robe—the ornate robe he was wearing." - **Genesis 37:23***

1. **Documenting Processes:** Just as Joseph stored grain during times of plenty, entrepreneurs must document their business processes, strategies, and intellectual property. This information helps ensure a smooth transition and operational continuity post-exit.

2. **Building Value:** In the parable of the talents, each servant was expected to increase the value of their resources. Entrepreneurs must focus on increasing the value of their business by optimizing operations, expanding customer base, and enhancing brand equity.

Personal Testimony: Closing One Chapter, Opening Another

In my own journey of exit planning, I recognized the importance of thoughtful preparation. As I explored different exit strategies, I focused on building a strong financial foundation, documenting key processes, and enhancing the value of my business. This attention to detail allowed for a seamless transition that ensured the legacy of my business continued under new ownership. Just as closing one chapter paves the way for the next, exit planning marks the end of one entrepreneurial journey and the opening of new possibilities.

In Conclusion

Exit planning marks the culmination of an entrepreneur's journey and the beginning of new opportunities. By exploring various exit strategy options, ensuring financial stability, and preparing the business for transition, entrepreneurs secure the legacy of their hard work. Just as authors conclude a book while leaving room for a sequel, entrepreneurs exit their businesses while paving the way for continued success and impact. Through strategic exit planning, entrepreneurs ensure that their business's story lives on even as they embark on new adventures.

Chapter 16:

Leaving a Lasting Impact

Planting Seeds of Legacy: Creating a Positive Impact

Just as a farmer plants seeds for future generations, entrepreneurs must create a positive legacy for their business and community. This chapter delves into leaving behind a meaningful impact through philanthropy, responsible business practices, and community engagement.

"For which of you, intending to build a tower, does not sit down first and count the cost, whether he has enough to finish it?" - **Luke 14:28**

1. **Philanthropy and Giving Back:** Like a generous giver who receives bountifully, entrepreneurs can contribute to causes that align with their values. Philanthropy not only benefits the community but also builds a positive reputation for the business.

2. **Responsible Business Practices:** Just as the good Samaritan demonstrated compassion, entrepreneurs must operate their businesses responsibly. Ethical practices, environmental sustainability, and social responsibility contribute to a positive legacy.

Mentoring the Next Generation: Passing the Torch

In the story of Elijah passing the mantle to Elisha, mentors pass down wisdom and knowledge. Entrepreneurs have the opportunity to mentor the next generation of entrepreneurs, fostering innovation and growth.

"Elijah said to Elisha, 'Tell me, what can I do for you before I am taken from you?' 'Let me inherit a double portion of your spirit,' Elisha replied." - ***2 Kings 2:9***

1. **Mentorship and Guidance:** Just as Elisha sought to inherit Elijah's spirit, aspiring entrepreneurs seek mentorship. Entrepreneurs can share their experiences, insights, and lessons learned to guide the next generation on their journey.

2. **Legacy in Action:** The legacy of Jesus's teachings continues through his disciples. Similarly, entrepreneurs leave behind a legacy through the businesses they've built and the impact they've had on their communities.

Personal Testimony: Sowing Seeds of Impact

In my own entrepreneurial journey, I recognized the significance of creating a lasting impact. By engaging in philanthropy, adopting responsible practices, and mentoring aspiring entrepreneurs, I aimed to leave behind a legacy that extended beyond my business. Just as a farmer's legacy is seen in the crops that grow long after they've sown the seeds, my legacy is defined by the positive changes my business and actions have brought to the community and the lives I've influenced.

In Conclusion

Leaving a lasting impact is a noble endeavor that extends beyond business success. By fostering positive change through philanthropy, responsible practices, and mentorship, entrepreneurs contribute to their community and shape the next generation of business leaders. Just as a well-tended garden continues to bloom, an entrepreneur's legacy lives on through the positive ripples of their actions. Through these efforts, entrepreneurs enrich their own lives and create a legacy that stands as a testament to their values and aspirations.

Appendices:

A. Resources for Further Reading, Tools, and Templates

Recommended Books:

1. **"The Lean Startup"** by Eric Ries

2. **"Good to Great"** by Jim Collins

3. **"Zero to One"** by Peter Thiel

4. **"Start with Why"** by Simon Sinek

5. **"Mindset: The New Psychology of Success"** by Carol S. Dweck

6. **"The Innovator's Dilemma"** by Clayton Christensen

7. **"Built to Last"** by Jim Collins and Jerry Porras

8. **"The Art of Possibility"** by Rosamund Stone Zander and Benjamin Zander

9. **"Blue Ocean Strategy"** by W. Chan Kim and Renée Mauborgne

10. **"The E-Myth Revisited"** by Michael E. Gerber

Online Courses:

1. Coursera: *"Entrepreneurship Specialization"* by University of Pennsylvania

2. Udemy: *"Business Plan Bootcamp: Everything You Need to Know"*

3. LinkedIn Learning: *"Leadership and Management for Entrepreneurs"* by John McWade

Templates:

1. Business Plan Template: A comprehensive guide to structuring your business plan.

Business Plan Template

1. Executive Summary:

Provide a concise overview of your business, highlighting its mission, unique value proposition, target market, and key goals.

2. Company Description:

Explain the background of your business, its history, legal structure, and location. Describe your business's purpose and the problem it aims to solve.

3. Market Analysis:

Conduct research on your target market, industry trends, and competitors. Define your target customer segments and outline their needs and preferences.

4. Marketing and Sales Strategy:

Detail your marketing approach, including branding, pricing, distribution, and promotion. Explain how you will attract and retain customers.

5. Product or Service Line:

Provide comprehensive details about your products or services, including their features, benefits, and any intellectual property.

6. Financial Projections:

Present your financial forecasts, including sales projections, expenses, profits, and cash flow. Include a break-even analysis and funding requirements.

7. Operations and Management:

Describe your business operations, such as production, logistics, and supply chain management. Introduce key team members and their roles.

8. SWOT Analysis:

Analyze your business's strengths, weaknesses, opportunities, and threats. Highlight how you will capitalize on strengths and address weaknesses.

9. Competitive Analysis:

Compare your business to your main competitors. Identify your competitive advantages and how you plan to position yourself in the market.

10. Funding and Financial Needs:

Explain how you plan to finance your business, whether through personal savings, loans, investors, or other sources. Specify how the funds will be used.

11. Milestones and Timelines:

Set out the key milestones you aim to achieve and the estimated timelines for their completion. This helps track your progress.

12. Exit Strategy:

Outline your potential exit strategies, whether through acquisition, merger, or other means. Discuss your long-term vision for the business.

This template is just a starting point. Depending on the complexity of your business, you might need to include more details and specific information in each section. Remember that a business plan serves as a roadmap for your business's success, helping you stay focused on your goals and making informed decisions.

2. Financial Projections Template: A tool to help you forecast revenue, expenses, and profitability.

Certainly, here's a simplified example of a financial projections template that includes some key financial forecasts for a hypothetical business:

Financial Projections Template

1. Sales Forecast:

- Month 1: $10,000

- Month 2: $12,000

- Month 3: $15,000

- ...

2. Cost of Goods Sold (COGS):

- Direct Materials: $3,000

- Direct Labor: $2,000

- Other COGS: $1,500

- Total COGS: $6,500

3. Gross Profit:

- Gross Profit = Sales - COGS

- Month 1: $10,000 - $6,500 = $3,500

- Month 2: $12,000 - $6,500 = $5,500

- ...

4. Operating Expenses:

- Marketing and Advertising: $800

- Rent and Utilities: $1,200

- Salaries and Wages: $2,500

- Other Operating Expenses: $1,000

- Total Operating Expenses: $5,500

5. Operating Income (EBIT):

- Operating Income = Gross Profit - Operating Expenses

- Month 1: $3,500 - $5,500 = -$2,000

- Month 2: $5,500 - $5,500 = $0

- ...

6. Net Income:

- Net Income = Operating Income - Taxes

- Month 1: -$2,000 - $300 = -$2,300

- Month 2: $0 - $400 = -$400

- ...

7. Cash Flow Projection:

- Beginning Cash Balance: $10,000

- Cash Inflows (Sales, Loans, Investments): $10,000

- Cash Outflows (Operating Expenses, COGS, Taxes): -$8,800

- Ending Cash Balance: $11,200

8. Break-Even Analysis:

- Fixed Costs (Rent, Utilities, Salaries): $4,000

- Variable Costs per Unit: $2.50

- Selling Price per Unit: $15.00

- Break-Even Point (Units): Fixed Costs / (Selling Price - Variable Costs) = 400 units

Please note that this is a simplified example and the numbers are hypothetical. In a real business plan, you'd provide more detailed forecasts, consider factors like seasonality, and conduct a more thorough analysis of costs and revenues. Financial projections are crucial for understanding the financial health of your business, making informed decisions, and attracting potential investors or lenders.

3. Marketing Strategy Template: A framework for developing an effective marketing plan.

Certainly, here's a simplified example of a marketing strategy template that outlines the key components of a marketing plan for a hypothetical business:

Marketing Strategy Template

1. Target Audience:

Identify your ideal customer segments based on demographics, psychographics, and behaviors.

2. Unique Value Proposition (UVP):

Define what sets your product or service apart from competitors and why customers should choose you.

3. Branding:

Establish your brand identity, including logo, colors, tagline, and overall brand personality.

4. Pricing Strategy:

Determine your pricing approach, considering factors like costs, competition, and perceived value.

5. Product Positioning:

Describe how you want your product or service to be perceived in the minds of customers.

6. Distribution Channels:

List the channels through which you will deliver your product to customers (e.g., online, retail, direct sales).

7. Promotion Plan:

Outline your tactics for promoting your product, including advertising, public relations, and digital marketing.

8. Content Strategy:

Detail the type of content you'll create to engage your audience (blog posts, videos, social media posts).

9. Social Media Strategy:

Specify which social media platforms you'll use and how you'll engage and interact with your audience.

10. Email Marketing:

Explain your approach to building an email list, creating valuable content, and nurturing leads.

11. Sales Strategy:

Describe your approach to converting leads into customers, including sales techniques and customer relationship management.

12. Metrics and Analytics:

Identify key performance indicators (KPIs) to measure the success of your marketing efforts (e.g., conversion rates, website traffic).

13. Budget Allocation:

Allocate your marketing budget to various tactics and channels, considering their potential impact.

14. Timeline:

Create a timeline for your marketing activities, including launch dates and ongoing campaigns.

15. Monitoring and Adjustments:

Explain how you'll monitor your marketing performance and make adjustments based on data and insights.

Please note that this is a simplified example, and a real marketing strategy template would likely include more details, data, and specific action plans for each tactic. Your marketing strategy guides your efforts to reach and engage your target audience effectively, promote your product, and ultimately drive sales and business growth.

B. Case Studies of Successful Startups and Their Journeys

Case Study 1: Airbnb

Learn how Airbnb disrupted the hospitality industry and transformed the way people travel and find accommodations.

Case Study 1: Airbnb - Revolutionizing Hospitality

Introduction:

Airbnb, founded in 2008 by Brian Chesky, Joe Gebbia, and Nathan Blecharczyk, began as a way to help travelers find affordable accommodations during high-demand events. Little did they know, their platform would revolutionize the hospitality industry and redefine the way people travel.

The Disruption:

Traditional hotels dominated the lodging industry until Airbnb disrupted the status quo. By connecting homeowners with spare rooms, apartments, or entire homes to travelers seeking unique experiences, Airbnb offered a more personalized and authentic alternative to standard hotel stays.

Key Factors Behind Airbnb's Success:

1. **Sharing Economy:** Airbnb tapped into the sharing economy, allowing individuals to monetize their unused space and enabling travelers to enjoy more affordable and distinctive lodging options.

2. **Personalization:** Airbnb's listings varied from cozy cottages to luxurious penthouses, catering to a wide range of preferences and budgets. This personalization attracted travelers seeking tailored experiences.

3. **Trust and Reviews:** Through guest reviews and host profiles, Airbnb established a trust-based community where both hosts and guests could make informed decisions based on shared experiences.

4. **Local Immersion:** Airbnb encouraged travelers to immerse themselves in local neighborhoods and culture, fostering connections with hosts who often acted as guides.

5. **Technology:** The platform's user-friendly website and app made it easy for users to search, book, and manage their stays. The convenience of online bookings played a pivotal role in Airbnb's rapid growth.

Impact on the Industry:

1. **Market Share:** Airbnb's exponential growth challenged the dominance of traditional hotel chains, forcing them to adapt and incorporate elements of the Airbnb model.

2. **Regulation and Challenges:** The rise of Airbnb also sparked debates about regulations, taxation, and the impact on housing availability in certain cities.

3. **Economic Opportunity:** Airbnb provided additional income streams for hosts, bolstering local economies and helping individuals generate revenue from their properties.

Legacy and Future:

Airbnb not only transformed the travel industry but also established itself as a symbol of the sharing economy. It introduced a new way of experiencing destinations and created a platform where strangers could connect and build meaningful relationships.

Lessons for Entrepreneurs:

1. **Identify a Gap:** Airbnb identified a gap in the market for personalized and affordable lodging options.

2. **Disruptive Innovation:** They harnessed the power of technology to disrupt a traditional industry, offering a fresh approach to an age-old concept.

3. **User Experience:** Airbnb prioritized user experience, creating an intuitive platform that made booking accommodations seamless.

4. **Community Building:** Building a community of trust through reviews and profiles contributed to Airbnb's success.

Airbnb's journey showcases the potential for innovation to reshape industries and create lasting impacts on how people experience the world.

Case Study 2: Tesla

Explore how Tesla revolutionized the automotive industry by pioneering electric vehicles and sustainable energy solutions.

Tesla - Driving Sustainable Innovation

Introduction:

Founded in 2003 by Elon Musk, Martin Eberhard, Marc Tarpenning, JB Straubel, and Ian Wright, Tesla set out to prove that electric vehicles (EVs) could be more than just an environmental alternative to traditional cars. The company aimed to revolutionize the automotive industry and accelerate the world's transition to sustainable energy.

The Disruption:

Tesla disrupted the automotive industry by introducing high-performance electric vehicles that shattered preconceptions about EVs. Their flagship Model S, released in 2012, demonstrated that EVs could offer exceptional range, speed, and luxury without compromising on environmental consciousness.

Key Factors Behind Tesla's Success:

1. **Innovative Technology:** Tesla's electric powertrain and battery technology set it apart from traditional automakers, offering increased efficiency and performance.

2. **Supercharger Network:** Tesla invested in a network of fast-charging stations, addressing range anxiety and making long-distance travel feasible for electric vehicle owners.

3. **Design and Performance:** Tesla's emphasis on sleek design and impressive acceleration appealed to consumers seeking both sustainability and high-performance.

4. **Autonomous Driving:** Tesla's commitment to autonomous driving technology demonstrated its forward-thinking approach to transportation.

5. **Sustainability:** Beyond vehicles, Tesla expanded into energy solutions, including solar panels, home batteries, and grid-scale energy storage.

Impact on the Industry:

1. **EV Adoption:** Tesla's success influenced other automakers to invest in electric vehicle development, accelerating the adoption of EV technology.

2. **Technological Innovation:** Tesla's innovations spurred advancements in battery technology and electric powertrains across the industry.

3. **Environmental Awareness:** Tesla's focus on sustainability raised awareness about the potential of electric vehicles to reduce carbon emissions.

Legacy and Future:

Tesla's impact extends beyond vehicles, contributing to a global conversation about sustainable transportation and energy solutions. The company's innovations continue to shape the trajectory of the automotive industry, inspiring competitors to innovate and embrace electrification.

Lessons for Entrepreneurs:

1. **Bold Vision:** Tesla's audacious goal of transforming transportation and energy systems drove its innovation.

2. **Disruptive Innovation:** By creating a product that defied expectations, Tesla disrupted an established industry.

3. **Holistic Approach:** Tesla's approach extended beyond vehicles, addressing energy and sustainability challenges.

4. **Customer Experience:** Focusing on design, performance, and user experience can drive adoption of innovative technologies.

Tesla's journey showcases the power of combining innovation, sustainability, and bold vision to create a lasting impact on industries and the world's perception of what's possible.

C. Glossary of Entrepreneurship and Business Terms

1. **Bootstrapping:** Funding a business using personal savings or revenue generated by the business itself.

2. **Angel Investor:** An individual who provides financial backing to startups in exchange for ownership equity.

3. **SWOT Analysis:** An assessment of a business's strengths, weaknesses, opportunities, and threats.

4. **Pivot:** A strategic change in direction to adapt to new market conditions or customer needs.

5. **ROI (Return on Investment):** A measure of the profitability of an investment relative to its cost.

6. **Freemium:** A business model that offers a basic version of a product for free, with premium features available for a fee.

7. **Scale Up:** The process of expanding a business to reach a larger market and generate higher revenues.

8. **Exit Strategy:** A plan outlining how entrepreneurs will exit their business, such as through acquisition or IPO.

9. **Elevator Pitch:** A concise and compelling description of a business idea that can be delivered in a short time.

10. **B2B (Business-to-Business):** Transactions and relationships between businesses rather than between businesses and individual consumers.

11. **Market Segmentation:** Dividing a target market into smaller groups based on shared characteristics or needs.

12. **Intellectual Property:** Legal rights that protect creations of the mind, such as inventions, designs, and trademarks.

13. **Supply Chain:** The network of organizations and processes involved in producing and distributing goods and services.

14. **ROI (Return on Investment):** A measure of the profitability of an investment relative to its cost.

15. **Cash Flow:** The movement of money into and out of a business, indicating its financial health.

16. **Franchise:** A business model where an individual or company licenses the right to operate a branch of their business.

17. **Break-even Point:** The point at which total revenue equals total costs, resulting in no profit or loss.

18. **Liquidity:** The ability of a business to convert its assets into cash quickly without incurring substantial losses.

19. **Value Proposition:** The unique benefits and value that a product or service offers to customers.

20. **E-commerce:** The buying and selling of goods and services over the internet.

These appendices provide you with a wealth of resources, practical examples, and essential definitions to enhance your understanding of entrepreneurship and business concepts. From recommended books to case studies and a glossary of terms, these tools are designed to support your journey in building and growing a successful business.

www.ingramcontent.com/pod-product-compliance
Lightning Source LLC
Chambersburg PA
CBHW071936210526
45479CB00002B/711